Merry Christmas

Welcome to Santa's Christmas WORLD

D1737437

I invite you to join me on a Christmas road trip.

Make Santa's world more colorful !

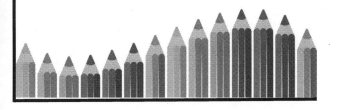
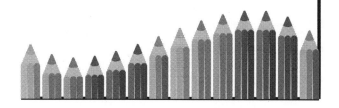

What else do you associate
with Christmas ?
Go ahead and draw !

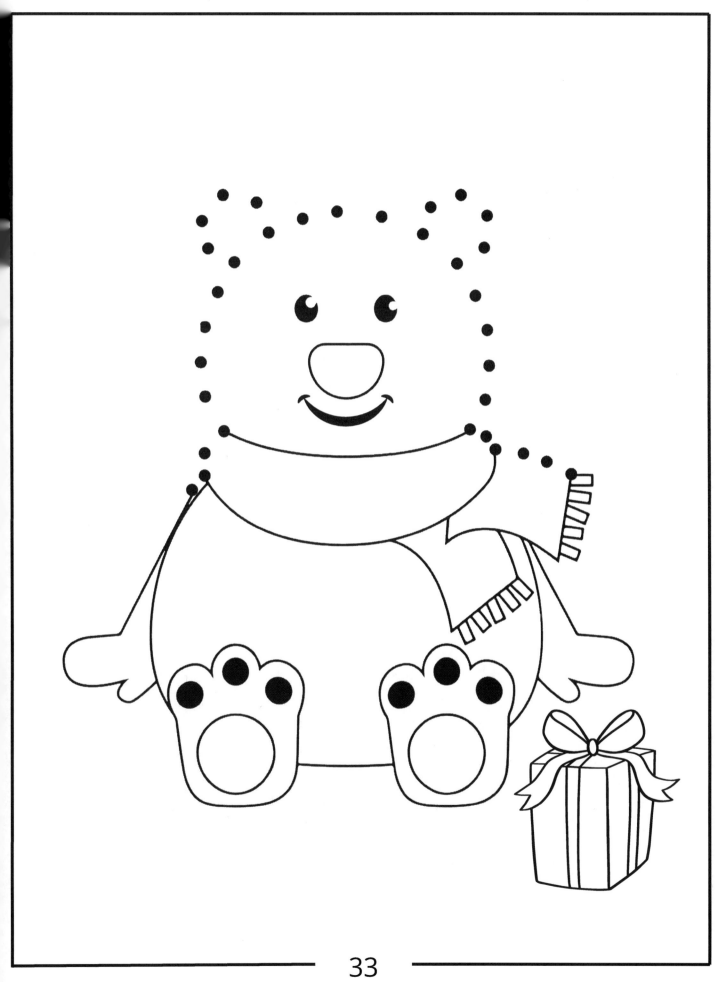

Decorate your Christmas wreath and tree

Create your dream bauble

Can you find 5 differences ?

Help Santa Claus find the bag with gifts.
Bring joy to all children in the world!

Make the presents find their way under the Christmas tree !

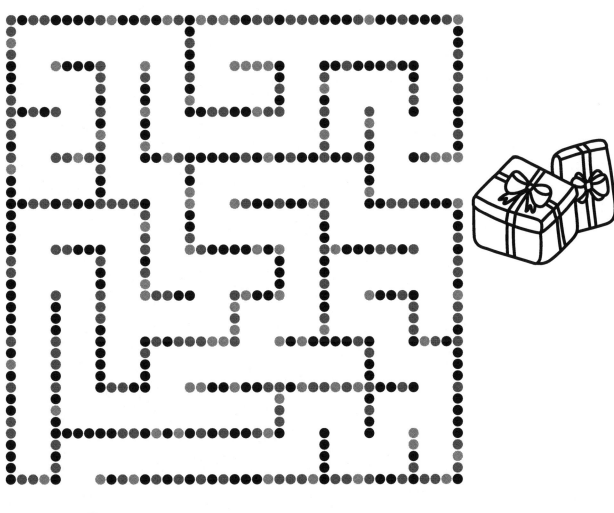

Will the Christmas elf find his way to the gifts?

MERRY CHRISTMAS

SANTA RIDES HIS SLEIGH SO BRIGHT,
THROUGH THE SNOW ON A STARRY NIGHT.
GIFTS FOR KIDS, BOTH BIG AND SMALL,
SMILES AND LAUGHTER FOR ONE AND ALL!

Made in the USA
Las Vegas, NV
04 December 2024

13314439R10063